Perils of Patriarchy

With
Candice Chirwa
Cassandra Moodley
Felicia Thobejane
Mila Goldberg
Milvia Iannantuoni
Nadine Hakizimana
Nokwanda Mpama
Sphilile Moyo
Thuli Nduvane
Yasaar Moosa

Published by Perils of Patriarchy 2019

Cover Design: Kayla De Freitas
Editor: Candice Chirwa
Proofreader: Ryan Meyer
Illustrations: Ellen Heydenrych
Johannesburg, South Africa

ISBN: 978-0-620-88014-5

Second Edition

**Dedication:
To all those fallen, to all those
surviving, to all those trying to
thrive.**

Perils of Patriarchy is an insightful and a necessary read. I identified with all the ten authors and have experienced and continue experiences most of what they have gone through. The book speaks so much on some of my wishes for women to narrate their own stories, using their own voices, at the own time and most importantly.

Philisiwe Mthimkulu- Educator and Activist

This book may well be the most well-concerted literary assault on patriarchy. It is bold, powerful, honest and fearless. South Africa has been waiting for a book like this, and now it's here.

Given Sigauqwe Communications & Strategic Information Specialist for Sonke Gender Justice

A collection of deep, moving, and intimate essays, reflecting the lived experience of womxn in a societal and cultural context that seeks to hold us down and violate us rather than uplift and celebrate us. Perils of Patriarchy is a thought-provoking, and important work.

Dr. Anastacia Tomson – Human Rights Defender, Medical Doctor and Author

Perils of Patriarchy is brilliant. With each and every story and chapter, I found a piece of myself. I could feel the women's thoughts and struggles. Perils of Patriarchy has opened up my eyes to yet another understanding of my brand of feminism.

I cried because I knew their pain.
I laughed because I got their jokes.
I agreed because I understood their journey.

Buhle Lupindo: Youtube Influencer and Content Creator

patriarchy

noun
1. a system of society or government in which
the father or eldest male is head of the family
and descent is reckoned through the male line.
"the thematic relationships of the ballad are
worked out according to the conventional
archetypes of the patriarchy"
    o   a system of society or government in
which men hold the power and women
are largely excluded from it.
    o   "the dominant ideology of patriarchy"
    o   a society or community organized on
patriarchal lines.
plural noun: **patriarchies**
"we live in a patriarchy"

P.S: The use of the word womxn/women is used
throughout this book. The term womxn which
originated in 1971 is an alternative word for women
to explicitly include all genders, transgender, and
people with marginalized genders. We as the
contributors want to be as inclusive as possible,
talking both to people who identify as women, no
matter biological sex and people who do not identify
as women.

The Perils

Authors Note
| Candice Chirwa

There are daily issues and struggles that womxn have to face; our freedom, dignity, safety and security. All of which are fundamental freedoms established by the democratic gains of 1994 which have not translated to the present day.

On paper, women in South Africa enjoy the highest status globally as our country boasts about a progressive Constitution as well as a legislative framework founded on the basis of human rights and gender equality. Yet, many womxn are frustrated as seen through various social media movements where feelings of hopelessness and inequality are expressed through the hashtag. The law exists, yes, but what practical function does it hold in society?

It is hard for people to understand the subtle things. Patriarchy or more over, male privilege, is one of the most contested topics that we struggle to grapple with as a nation and is something we cannot communicate honestly and openly about.

I have attended enough workshops, talks and protests to come to terms with the fact that we as a country are still struggling to deal with the societal norms that womxn and men face. And yes men are included in this. We have to acknowledge that patriarchy is the most life-threatening social disease assaulting the male body. By definition, patriarchy is a political-social system insistent on males inherently dominating, superior to everything and everyone deemed weak, especially females, thus leaving men endowed with the right to dominate and rule over the 'weak' to maintain their power.

This power is seen in different settings. At work, school, the nightclub, the list of venues is endless. Men's role in society is to be served, to provide, to be strong, to think, strategize and plan. We are aware of these roles which men are expected to fulfil, but as a society, we do not reflect on those who don't? How does society attack the outlier, the un-alpha male? We as womxn need to have more conversations about how we can be the gatekeepers and perpetrators of the very social system we are trying to break.

Further, in as much as society is quick to blame men, it is important to acknowledge the limitations of freewill men have from birth.

In general, when men have been indoctrinated into the patriarchy, they are expected to feel no pain and to deny their emotions. It is up to men to self-inspect as to how they engage with this social disease. It must be accepted that the tyrannical power of patriarchy still holds all of us captive. Thus, the first step in self-inspection is understanding how the social system has impacted all of us. There are many womxn who have personal stories that will make you question the society you share, with not enough being done to address the failure of our society to hold perpetrators to account. I hope that these ten stories from ten brave womxn sharing their Perils of Patriarchy will make you self-inspect, self-reflect and most importantly, unlearn for the sake of building a better society.

P.S: This book is a tool on how to co-exist. This book in no way an attack on men. But rather an invitation for us to create a better society for a better generation. I hope that by reading this book, it can spark the necessary conversations needed for societal change. We as contributors hope that our personal experiences will create a society where womxn will be able to experience the true meaning of freedom.

Peril One: Right of Admission Reserved
| Sphilile Moyo

"The enemy is not men. The enemy is the concept of patriarchy, the concept of patriarchy as the way to run the world"
- Toni Morrison

When I was eight I refused to play with other children because he molested me

When I was ten he smashed my head against the bathroom door

Later that day I laid on the floor contemplating ways of killing myself

When I was twelve I surrendered myself to the Lord and promised to serve him

When I was 15 a Priest forced Himself on to me

Later that day I fell on my knees but refused to pray

After prayer times I was told how stupid I am for not praising God, the same God who allowed a man to force himself on me.

When I was sixteen I drank 100 pills

I wanted to die and go to hell for my body was never mine and will never be mine

My body belonged to God's favourite people, they can use it anyhow and discard it however

My body was a temple for men to destroy their leisure

When I was eighteen, a male friend asked me who will marry a fat girl like me

I spent years shrinking myself, swallowing my emotions the same way I swallowed patriarchy

Laugh like a lady

Walk like a lady

Sleep like a lady

I hated my body, the way I laughed and my whole existence

When I was twenty, I realized I have been groomed to please men

In a perfect world where we are all God abiding being

I would be a chess piece to be controlled by men

When I was twenty two I found Freedom

When I was 22 I found Feminism

I fell in love with my body and the way I laugh until tears run down my cheeks

I fell in love with the woman I am

Who isn't afraid to shake patriarchy

Who isn't afraid to disrupt misogyny

Who will never be afraid of being called the angry black feminist

Within me there is a fire that my mother gave me and the fire that her mother gave her

And all the fire of all the women in my bloodline
Praised be to Feminism.

Peril Two: Feminism in Practice
| Yasaar Moosa

"I have chosen to no longer be apologetic for my femaleness and my femininity. And I want to be respected in all of my femaleness because I deserve to be."
- Chimamanda Ngozi Adichie

In my life, I have been absolutely blessed with strong women and extremely understanding men. That is not to say that I have never experienced acts of male dominance because that's impossible to escape in today's society. However, I have been equipped with the intuition to know my achievements are equal and as valid as anyone else with the same, but this becomes challenging when the system favours one group over another.

Nevertheless, my mindset will not change. I have always been obsessed with strong women, going far beyond their presence in my life. This obsession started early in my high school journey when I found an affinity for royalty, specifically Queens. History made this easy because there are so few queens who get the recognition they deserve. Four Queens stand out amongst the pages of men, Cleopatra, Hatshepsut, Elizabeth I and Mary Queen of Scots. Interestingly enough, all four Queens used their femininity in different ways to flourish in male dominated societies and all of whom were ultimately destroyed by men.

For Hatshepsut, she had to develop a more masculine identity in order for her reign to be viewed as a legitimate ruler, this was accomplished by wearing masculine clothing, including a beard traditionally worn by male Pharos, however, after her death, most of her legacy was destroyed as her reign was viewed as illegitimate. For Cleopatra, she used her femininity as a weapon, her beauty, charm and sex appeal are often how she was able to easily manipulate men. For Queen Elizabeth and Queen Mary, ruling during the same era but in different regions, being the only legitimate heirs to the throne. Due to the male influences in their lives Elizabeth and Mary turned on each other believing that they were enemies which ultimately lead to Elizabeth executing Mary for treason.

Both Queens had immense power and were therefore feared because of it, thus the men around them conspired to both of their downfalls. Ironically, they were completely opposite, as Elizabeth developed a more dominant and hypermasculine exterior similar to that of

Egyptian Queen Hatshepsut, whereas Queen Mary followed in the footsteps of Cleopatra, in the sense that she relied on her charm and beauty, even though both Queens were extremely intelligent. It seems that women have always been forced to adapt into a male dominated society though assimilation, rather than being accepted through their own merits. Women are either forced to be hypermasculine in order to be recognized or they need to oversexualize themselves to gain attention.

This is a trend I see mirrored in women today, either using their hypersexuality as a tool for their advantage or adopting overly masculine traits in order to fit into male dominated society. This led me to the question, are strong women born? Or are they created?

Personally, I would like to think that all women are born strong, however, I believe that strong women are created. This is done through the many hardships that we face on a daily basis. In the same way, a series of unfortunate events may change you forever, it ultimately makes sure you never repeat the same sequence of events.

Women are bi-products of their circumstances, however, these circumstances should not define who we are. Women are forced to create a persona reserved for the outside world, a brave face, forced to wear out of necessity each and every day. Walking down the street, entering a room, ordering a coffee, browsing a book shop, engaging with men, dealing with male co-workers. It's a face women seldomly forget at home.

The title of Chimamanda Ngozi Adichie book, *We Should All be Feminists* got me thinking, why is everyone not a feminist and where does patriarchy stem from? Okay let's be real, for the most part, physically, men are stronger than women, it is just genetics. Millennia ago, brute strength was necessary for survival and because women were perceived to be weaker, it made sense for men to be the protectors and leaders. However, in the modern age, strength is not a defining characteristic of leadership, rather Chimamanda cites, creativity, intelligence, innovation and rationality are the new characteristics for leadership and none of those are determined by one's hormones. Therefore, women are just as qualified as men. So why are women not afforded the same opportunities as men? Like many things in this world including turning books into movies, the zombie apocalypse and New Year's resolutions, some things are just better in theory. But feminism is something that we actively need to practice in mundane tasks. Feminism in practice is not assigning blame but rather an equilibrium that we need to strive towards, not only between men and women but between all kinds (should I used the word **intersections**) of women. In the case of Queen Elizabeth and Queen Mary, rather than tearing each other down and falling into the rumours, they should have united and presented a stronger force. When women stand together, we are truly unstoppable.

One of the most profound quotes from the book *We Should All Be Feminists* is how author Chimamanda Ngozi Adichie defines feminism for herself. She states that she is "a Happy African Feminist Who Does Not Hate Men and Who Likes to Wear Lip Gloss and High Heels for

Herself and Not For Men". This stood out for me because it's funny how there are so many labels and negative connotations associated with feminism, so many that Chimamanda had to explicitly specify which type of feminist she associates as. Feminism and feminists are often stereotypically depicted as women who hate men, therefore, Chimamanda states that she is a happy feminist who doesn't hate men. This idea of being a happy feminist originates from the idea that feminism is a Western concept therefore, it is not African, thus Chimamanda states she is a happy feminist. The last part of the quote mentions that she enjoys wearing lip gloss and high heels for herself and not men, for me this is important. In today's society, the female body is hypersexualized and viewed as an object for the male gaze, therefore, making the distinction that wearing certain clothing items and make up is for your own enjoyment rather than that of a male is so important.

A story that I am very familiar with is the one of the first few years of my parent's marriage. My mom got married at the age of 21, placing her in the final year of university. My dad already completed his qualification by marriage. My mom fell pregnant with me the following year while she completed her honours degree and my dad took the opportunity to make sure everything on the home front was taken care of, so that my mother could focus on academia whilst pregnant. Once my mom completed her qualification, she took a break and gave my dad a chance to study further. And they did this cycle until my mom got her PhD. I remember as a young girl listening to this story about team work, equality and respect thinking to myself this is what a marriage, a partnership is all about. Allowing each other to shine individually in order to collectively flourish. If one of my parents was selfish during this time, in the sense that they both decided to pursue their academic careers the family and home aspect of their relationship would have failed. For me this was and still is a perfect example of balance and equality. For me the definition of equality and feminism overlap so much in the sense that equality is understood as men and women being treated the same within a social, political and economic setting and the exact same thing can be said about feminism. Women globally are striving for equal recognition in all aspects of life.

That is why the notion of feminism is so weird for me because I thought inherently everyone was a feminist because that was my experience. I always wondered who wouldn't want equality? I have always believed in the notion of feminism, for me, feminism is equality of the sexes, point blank, period. The idea that men and women should be treated equality within all spheres of life, based on the fact that we are all human. Finding out that not everyone shares this belief, for me, was incomprehensible.

With that in mind, my family has always valued religion. My father states that in his religion (Islam), the Quran dictates that females should be treated equally to that of their counterparts (men). By virtue of being a feminist, my father believes that it is degrading to women, to being treated special rather than equally. Shocked and concerned I asked him to define what feminism meant to him? Well this is the response I got, "females must have the right to be able to do certain things. Feminism says that women should be able to earn equal salary women must have an equal spacing sport and so on". For me it goes further because equality is one of those concepts that are great in theory, but rarely get practiced in day to day life.

Equality is good and all, but access might be better. In the sense that if the entering of political, social and economic space was accessible to women this would lead to freedom for women to enter these spaces, thus leading to equality. Therefore, equality, access and freedom should go hand in hand in helping society make progress.

In that sense, my father always says that men and women are equal but different, citing their physical differences, including the notion that men are stereotypically stronger than women, yet women have the ability to give birth and men do not. Regardless, this does not make one more superior than the other but rather different. Diversity is always a good thing; diversity breeds change, new ideas and advancements, society cannot evolve without diversity. Stagnant pools of water are breeding grounds for diseases and infections and if we apply stagnation to society it creates a system in which corruption and oppression become the norm.

Therefore, when something new is introduced it seems threatening. 400 years ago, women ruling an entire nation seemed like lunacy, 100 years women were not allowed to vote and 25 years ago women of colour were allowed to vote in South Africa. Only 40 years ago the first female president was elected in Iceland and in 2018, only three countries had 50%+ representation of women in parliament. However, like fresh and flowing water, 'the new' attracts diversity in many different forms which can be highly beneficial to society.

Personally, I view change as a two-sided coin. On the one end is the scary unknown and on the other side, is the new and beneficial. And like a coin, all sides of humanity need to come together in order to move forward. Regardless, change is inevitable whether we like it or not.

Peril Three: Toxic Feminity
| Mila Goldberg

That is disgusting!
(The Greek Chorus rises in my head – a susurrus
of shame – *You are disgussssssting*)
    I do not know whose voice it is anymore…
Mine or theirs.
I was told that it is what women do
what they MUST do
Because they…we…are women.

    I was 12 when I watched a friend as she did
it. How she let the blades slide over the
contours, hand hanging limply above her head as
she focused intensely on the barely-there-fluff
    under
    her
    arms
A barely-there-fluff that had yet to appear under
mine.
    When she offered me the razor, I took hold
of it
    Nonchalant
    After all, hesitation or refusal could show
my isolation from the land of women
    I have a vagina

Hear my muffled roar
That is disgusting

My mother could not know the
damage
She caused
She passed down her mother's-mother's-
mother's wisdom,
Passed down by the wisdom of those, who
know better than I,
That I can still be The Best A Man Can Get
If I pluck and prune
Disgusssssssting

And ignore the rash
the itch
the welts
the shame

I decided to stop the plucking and pruning
The rash   itch   welts
Not before asking a man who I love if he
could love what my body is
Disgusssssssting

And still I hear the voice.
    I cannot be the Best for a Man
    I am…
Disgussssssting

    …not what they want

    I convinced myself that I would rather be
    Clean
    Pure
    The Best
Disgussssssting

    I could not find support in women
    My mother
    My sister
Disgussssssting

    The voice in my head
    Mine
    or
    Theirs?

I have let my barely-there-fluff go
(let myself go?)
And grow

But still I inspect the damage
Do I remain a woman
if I am not the
Best A Man Can Get?
Disgussssssting

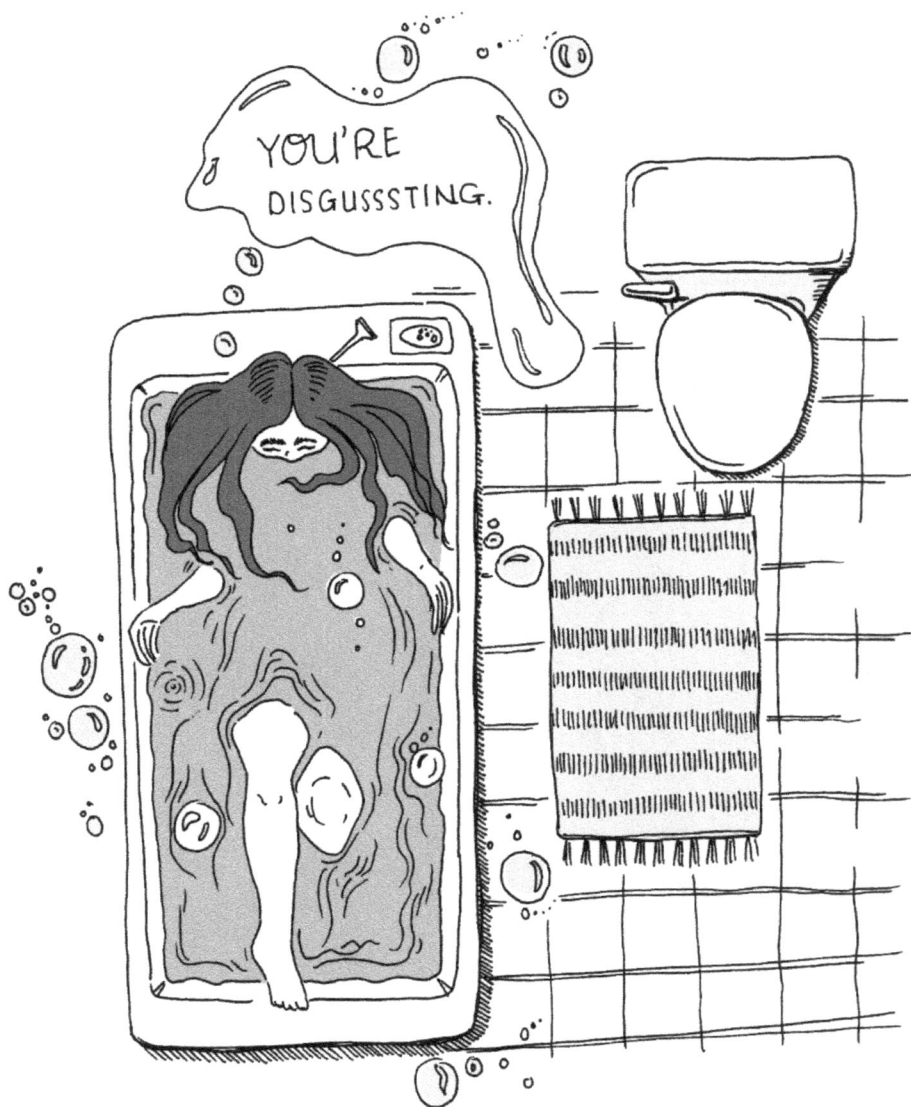

Peril Four: Beauty is Patriarchal
| Nadine Hakizimana

"Beauty begins the moment you decide to be yourself"
- Coco Chanel

"Behind every beautiful thing, there's been some kind of pain"
- Bob Dylan

Can you imagine the awkward experience of being a black woman and having to ask a Bangladeshi man, who owns one of your favourite hair shops for advice on the best brand of hairpiece for your braids? Perhaps you could imagine the confusion of looking for make-up for an event and instead being offered skin-bleaching cream by a Chinese man? Or watching a white European man come to collect rent from all the hairdressers - who have barely had any clients that day, in the salon where you get your hair done?

I don't have to imagine it because I have lived it and I know that many other black women and girls can resonate with these scenarios. There is big business in black beauty; it is a multi-billion dollar industry but hardly any of that money makes it back to the black community. I get my hair done in the central business district of Pretoria. Anyone who has ever bought beauty products in that area would have noticed that the industry in Pretoria is dominated by Asian businessmen who profit off of products targeted at black women. Just one look at the back of popular hair products, hair extensions, skin cream or make-up in black beauty supply stores will reveal that the majority of them are made by Chinese, Korean or Indian manufacturing companies owned by men.

If one were to take it a step further to inquire about the land or infrastructure that hosts many black beauty businesses, or to whom the rent is paid, it would not be surprising to see that a white male is the main benefactor. My take is that the predominance of men in the black beauty industry is part of a much broader and much more sinister agenda than many of us may assume. As such, this chapter exposes the perils of patriarchy found in the black beauty industry from the perspective of a young black African woman in South Africa.

Before delving into the nitty gritty of the issue at hand, allow me to introduce myself. I am Nadine Hakizimana - Rwandese by blood, Botswana-born and South Africa-raised. It might also be a good time to mention that I love to wear make-up, I love to change up my hairstyles and I love experimenting with fashion. It's safe to say I am a quintessential girly-girl. Beauty matters to me because it is an expression of my personal identity, my feminine prowess and a source of my confidence, but it is also an extension of my cultural identity because there are unspoken beauty expectations that come with being a Rwandese woman or "umunyarwandakazi" as my countrymates would say. However, spending the majority of my life in Botswana and South Africa, I was faced with having to navigate standards of beauty that are completely different to what I look like. Traits that are considered to be the norm in Rwanda very often were deemed exotic - not always in a good way... both in Botswana and in South Africa. I mention all these characteristics because my experience of patriarchy is inextricably tied, not only to my experience of being a woman, but also to my experience of blackness and my experience of foreignness.

Through my experience, I have come to understand beauty as a form of romantic, social and professional capital that can buy your way into different types of relationships and endeavours, it's almost like a transactional exchange. It can be exchanged for different benefits of life like marriage, a friend or a dream job but it is something which is established by patriarchy - which renders women as mere entertainment for men and white supremacy - which governs the mainstream standards of what can and cannot be considered beautiful. When one understands that beauty confers societal advantages, spending loads of money to look beautiful becomes an easy decision. In fact, I get my hair done at a salon at least 8 times a year. On average, I could spend a minimum of R700 each time - bringing the total to roughly R5 600 a year. Let's not even get started on what I spend annually on skincare products, make-up and clothes. As difficult as it may be to admit, I don't think I would spend so much money on my appearance if I did not believe it would favour my romantic, social and professional prospects. The questions then become: what standard of beauty do I need to follow in order to reach my desired goal? Who are the gatekeepers of said beauty? It appears as though the business model of the beauty industry is to induce feelings of insecurity and then promote beauty products as the solution to that insecurity, in order to continue selling all these products. I refer to beauty as a game in this sense because the moment you attain it, the standard changes. In this way, you are constantly spending your money while chasing an ever-changing ideal that you can never reach because it is a function of capitalism, patriarchy, and racism.

The message that this sends is that you are not acceptable the way you are naturally.

I am a melanated sistah and I've actually fallen victim to this capitalist, patriarchal, business ploy. I was made to feel insecure about my skin colour when I was just 18 years old. I never thought twice about the darkness of my skin until I was offered skin-whitening cream in the weeks leading up to my matric dance in 2013. While I was extremely shocked and offended by this suggestion, I later learned that skin-whitening cream is one of the most popular products on the African continent. The high supply suggests to us that there is a high demand. If we think about it in this way, then the onus is actually on the consumers, who may feel like their skin colour is inadequate for their specific goal.

If you ask me, the constant desire to buy more in order to enhance beauty is less about self-hate and more about women who are trying to find empowerment and agency in an oppressive, patriarchal system. Women respond by navigating this system through beauty consumerism. There are women who truly feel the need to chase this fleeting, ever-changing standard of beauty in order to survive the game of life. Even though a part of me believes my efforts for beauty represent a conquest for power, I would be negligent if I didn't recognize that this endeavour happens within an oppressive patriarchal system. One cannot discount the consideration of the male-gaze when making decisions about enhancing beauty. I have noticed that beauty does confer societal advantages. With the recognition of this fact, it is easy to understand why women may go the extra mile for the societal reward.

However, in acknowledging the pressure to entertain the male-gaze, we also need to be careful not to erase black women's agency. Part of the reason why I enjoy being a black woman, is the ability to change my image as often as I see fit - I could wear a weave one month and the next rock my Afro. In this way, I am able to have a spectrum of experiences because I feel like a new person with each new hairstyle - like I said earlier, beauty forms part of my personal identity. This is one of the ways in which I navigate the patriarchal order that is imposed on black beauty.

It may sound contradictory to speak about the pain of beauty because it is largely assumed that beauty can only confer societal advantages. However, a closer, more critical inspection of beauty reveals that it is not problem-free. There are in fact very real and painful issues that come with being beautiful or having pressure to conform to a standard of beauty that diverts from who you are naturally. Conversations about beauty are often watered down to superficial narratives that ignore the complexities of the social, professional and economic engagement with beauty. The fact that a beautiful woman can be scolded by her boss for being a distraction to the men in her workplace, or the fact that some women feel the need to spend exorbitant amounts of money in order to survive in certain settings, are part of the problem.

The message that I take from my personal experiences of beauty, some of which I have mentioned here is that there are multiple forces all working together to pressurize women to look a certain way. These are my experiences but I know many other women can resonate with them. It is a constant battle that cannot be resolved with songs motivating us to love ourselves the way we are, or feminist marches packed with women with hairy armpits in an attempt to be non-conformist. We need to be honest about the duality of our perspectives of beauty. If you ask me, I'd encourage you to stop seeing beauty as a shallow, superficial characteristic. In the same breath I would also encourage you to question consumerist enterprises that jump at any opportunity to capitalize on your insecurities. There is nothing wrong with liking fancy things, the problem only arises when you would rather be your natural self but feel pressured to alter yourself in order to advance in romantic, social or professional pursuits.

Peril Five: Moving Violation
| Candice Chirwa

"Being a womxn in South Africa is proving to be somewhat of an extreme sport."
- Katlego Modise

Do you ever wonder why womxn insist on going to the bathroom with a friend? It is not partly because we are secretly plotting the demise of patriarchy. It is because our safety is not guaranteed. Ask any group of womxn if they've ever felt unsafe on public transportation? And their stories will flow.

Of course, womxn can't be treated as an undifferentiated group. Disability, class, race, age, sexuality, gender, presentation, and other factors mean that not all womxn are equally vulnerable to crime or violence on public transportation. Men and boys can also be victimized and it should not be assumed that every womxn is a victim-in-waiting. The truth is, womxn do experience a large amount of harassment and abuse while traveling alone. As children, it was drilled into our heads to never get into a car with a stranger. Fast forward to the 21st century, and now it is something we do with little hesitation. We rarely think twice when using an app for a stranger to give us a ride to the airport or a ride home after a fun night out.

I did not think twice on the 22nd of December, 2016 when I was coming back from a friends' birthday party in Muldersdrift. The joyous occasion was filled with love, light, and laughter. Eventually, as the night went on, the thought came up: "*I need to get home*" and I had decided to use the popular e-hailing app - Uber. All I remember about that night was that I did nothing but say no to the driver from the first minute. Nothing out of my mouth was ever anything other than no.

"*Would you like the aircon on?*"

    No.

"*Is there a specific route you'd like for me to take?*"

    No.

"*Would you like for me to change the radio station?*"

    No.

The ride started off professional and slowly started turning into a triggering conversation.

"*Do you have a boyfriend?*"

    No.

"*You look nice, Can I take you out sometime?*"

No.
"Are you interested in me?"
No.
"How about I stop on the side of the road until
you agree to go out with me?"
No, Please, No.

All it took was three taps on my phone to request a ride. All I wanted was a safe ride home, in the end, all I received was emotional trauma.

Reminiscing on that drive, I recall that the only thing that flashed in my mind was all the stories I had come across on social media about womxn being in scary situations, in an effort to just get home.

About 56% of South Africans depend on public transport to get to work, to go out for social activities and to visit their families. Womxn especially those traveling alone, are increasingly vulnerable when using public transport. There have been too many incidents that have been reported of womxn being assaulted while using public transport. And if you don't believe me, simply type in your browser: "Public Transport

Horror Stories South Africa" and you will be astounded to see the multiple stories that have been documented.

And if you still don't believe me, then indulge me with your time and reflect on the nuances that womxn face when going out. We as womxn, have to make meticulous decisions about our clothing, document our movements to friends and family members by sharing our live location when we do go out. Society perpetuates the message that safety from sexual harassment and violence is solely our responsibility. Public transport providers further perpetuate this message by advising commuters to regulate their behaviour to stay safe. Tips include: "Keep a protective device"; "Be aware of your surroundings"; "Do not attract attention, wear modest clothing." It would be refreshing for an article to inform society not to rape or attack passengers instead, the question I ask myself is *WHOSE FAULT IS IT?*

Really, what I am saying is that womxn are not the problem. Yet society tends to make it seem like it is. Womxn are constantly debating whether we have the right to speak, the right to go out, the right to exist. We constantly have to monitor what we say, and our choice of words, whether we are sitting or are we standing. *If we are sitting, how are sitting, are my legs too open*, and *if we are standing, then what are we wearing*? When we speak, we need to consider whether our voices are pitched just right to understand whether we will be taken seriously in a conversation.

Think about the mental gymnastics we as womxn have to do in order to have a conversation, in order to travel to places, in order to just be. And now imagine what it would be like if we lived in a world where we didn't have to do anything of that. Where we can just speak, travel and just live. All I want is to stop living in a world where we are second class citizens and our only job is it to make men comfortable.

I am part of a private Facebook group for womxn in South Africa and recently, someone started a thread about her experience being harassed on public transport. Suddenly, dozens of other womxn joined in on the conversation, sharing their own stories. Here are some of the comments that were shared:

> *"I've gotten harassed plenty on the bus, and it's always degrading, embarrassing and sometimes terrifying."*

> *"I once had a guy follow me off the bus and literally chase me after me for my number after politely declining."*

> *"The last time I was assaulted was the final time I used a taxi. I couldn't take it anymore."*

This is what womxn are up against. Every day. Most days go smoothly, but there are also the days when someone won't leave you alone and you start to get worried. You have to be constantly on the lookout, especially at night. I am trying to envision a society where womxn will be able to walk, drive and travel without the thought of "Will this be my last day? Will I make it home safely?".

When I choose to have children, am I expected to relive the trauma of the 22nd of December 2016? Having to explain to my girl child the potential dangers that exist due to a social system that leaves men to be entitled over womxn's bodies? Am I expected to relive, explaining to my girl child, how public transport operators will fail to provide answers for the ride that ended with emotional trauma rather than a destination?

If you are still reading this chapter, and you still do not understand this peril, then allow this chapter to be a conversation starter with family and friends. I hope you understand that for many womxn, the immediate "solution" to harassment is to avoid eye contact with others, to travel in pairs, and to always live on high alert. It should not have to be this way.

Traveling is a freedom. Travelling has no gender. We as womxn, want to travel alone without fear of being punished for it.

Peril Six: Men Unimagined
| Nokwanda Mpama

"Like a compass needle that points north, a man's accusing finger always finds a woman. Always"
- Khaled Hosseni

My name is Nokwanda Mpama and I am a final year LLB student at the University of the Witwatersrand. When I was approached to write a chapter in this book, I jumped at the opportunity not only to explore writing outside of a legal context, but I also saw this as a chance to introspect and really think about my experiences with men. If you ask any woman about their experiences with masculinity, they'll probably be able to relay a story to you without much thought or hesitation. I on the other hand, really had to think. To be honest, I don't think about men and I don't recall ever being completely enamoured with a man. In order to write this chapter, I had to reach deep into the recesses of mind and ponder who men are to me. I want this chapter to be more than the thoughts of a charming but slightly awkward girl in the middle of an existential crisis. I want to put forward a different perspective to a longstanding discussion. This is not the first book to discuss patriarchy and its dire effects and I hope to God that it isn't the last. The absence of novelty does not by any means equate to a lack of importance. Every chapter in this book brings with it a significant insight into the lived experiences of each woman and I hope my mine will aid in conveying the complexities of masculinity and patriarchy.

My first experiences of masculinity are very positive. I'm fortunate to have incredible memories of growing up around strong, empathetic and phenomenal men. The first man that comes to mind naturally is my father. He is one of the most loving and dependable people I have ever known. In a house full of women, he never had to assert himself as the head of the household. He expresses his masculinity through love and leads with compassion. Another man that comes to mind is my uncle. He would put me on his shoulders, and we'd walk around the neighbourhood and visit his friends, all of whom I still hold in high esteem. I also have a cousin whom I adore. He is the wittiest and most intelligent person in my life, he is not like other men I've come across. He possesses a gentleness and a level of approachability that a lot of men I've encountered lack. He serves as a reminder that men can be as multi-dimensional as they want to be.

My dad's friends also come to mind when I think of incredibly influential men. My dad has been part of a burial society since before my sister and I were born and every couple of years, they have their members meeting at my house. Although the idea of being around 30 men over the age of 60 would be insufferable to some, I absolutely love having them around. These men are father figures that exemplify what it means to be a man. None of these men are perfect by any stretch of the imagination but they understand that being a man is more than overt displays of bravado. I'm not sure if it comes with age but my dad's friends all seem at ease with themselves and don't need to impress anyone. I find the most dangerous men are those who feel like they have something to prove.

Just to digress slightly, I'd like to very briefly discuss violent men. Men who carry with them a weak sense of masculinity assert themselves in the most ferocious ways. Recently the term 'fragile masculinity' has been coined to describe such men. You'll see posts on social media or hear people say, "Oh he suffers from fragile masculinity". I don't really agree with this. I don't want to overcomplicate things but for me, the word "suffer" implies an affliction of some sort. I think the idea that the abhorrent violence some men show toward women can merely be attributed to a case of fragile masculinity is an oversimplification of a bigger problem and it allows these men to escape accountability.

Men are angry for a multitude of reasons and at times that anger manifests into violence. Many are raised to believe that fragility of any kind is completely incompatible with manhood and that any challenge to their masculinity should be met with the most visceral anger. I don't believe that men are inherently violent or predatory, I think such behaviour is taught and as society, we must figure out how to deal with it. I would also like to express my disaffection with our government. The recent spate of femicide and increased gender-based violence has not resulted in action from the government. I don't mean to offend anyone but marches, moments of silence and speeches in parliament do not make women feel heard. Without implementation and funding of safety programmes, femicide will continue to be one of many unfortunate things that happen in South Africa, like corruption.

I can guarantee that come election season, a political party will have the audacity to use women being killed and gender-based violence as part of campaign for votes. We need a complete reconstruction of our beliefs about gender and how we raise children. The day men stop treating women as objects will be the day our lives truly begin. Until then, being a woman in South Arica is an extreme sport, an incredibly dangerous terrain to navigate.

Anyway, back to my story.

My high regard for men started to wane when they began seeing me as a sexual conquest. I hate it when men flirt with me, not only does it make me uncomfortable, but the lack of ingenuity irks me. I'm not sure if this a common issue throughout the continent but South African men don't know how to flirt. If only one South African man reads this chapter, please Chief, tell your friends to do better because I and many other women are highly unimpressed. I can't tell you how many times I've heard "I love you my sister" from absolute strangers in taxis and in different parts of town. I used to smile awkwardly and shuffle away. This response or lack thereof, was fuelled by fear because there are men in this world that don't take kindly to the word "no" and you don't know until you piss them off. Unfortunately, no man has the phrase "if you refuse my advances, I'll moer you" plastered on their face. However, about three years ago, I got over this fear and I started asking these "chivalrous" men: "What do you love about me?" Most of them give me a vacant look and are unable to answer because they have never been asked to explain themselves. Essentially, we live in a world where men don't have to explain themselves.

Many men I've encountered are not used to being held accountable for the things they say. Men speak without thinking and expect women to just smile and accept it. I believe that this is a consequence of society treating men as the ultimate authority figures in every space they occupy, from the household to the office, men are unquestionable. In fact, in Zulu culture, as in many African cultures, it's considered rude to look directly at man when speaking to him. When a self-assured woman who values her dignity, dares transgress these archaic social constructs by disagreeing or questioning a man, you hear some men accuse her of being disrespectful or will ask: "do you want to be the man in this household?" These responses have always intrigued me because they suggest that many men believe that respect and dignity are qualities reserved for men and any woman who wants to be treated with some semblance of dignity doesn't know her place.

I am not satisfied with merely burning my bra and vilifying men, the point of this chapter is to convey that not every woman's experience with masculinity is unilaterally negative. Men are complicated, multi-faceted beings who just happen to be protected by patriarchy. I am also well aware of the fact that there will be multiple definitions of patriarchy put forth by the exceptional ladies that have contributed to this book, but please bear with me as I attempt to put forth my own. I define patriarchy as the advancement and protection of men to the detriment of women. Patriarchy is inherently violent, exclusionary and dangerous. Countless of men rubbish the idea of patriarchy as pure fiction and a figment of the overactive feminist imagination. These men are unaware or choose to be complacent with patriarchy because it serves them. The adverse effects of patriarchy only become apparent to men when they act contrary to what this deeply entrenched social construct demands. Patriarchy in my view is different to masculinity. I don't know how I got this far into this chapter without attempting to define masculinity but here goes nothing: I would define masculinity as the expression of manhood. Like most human behaviour, I'd like to think that masculinity presents itself in many forms and as I have tried to illustrate, masculinity can be beautiful and extremely positive.

Many men and women conflate patriarchy with masculinity. This became evident when

#MenAreTrash started doing the rounds on social media, this was also when Karabo Mokoena was murdered by her boyfriend. What was particularly disturbing to me was the fact that men on my Facebook feed were more distressed about being likened to trash than the fact that a woman was murdered by her boyfriend who stuffed her body in a dustbin then set her on fire in an abandoned field. South Africa has the highest statistics of violent crimes against women and children. We have the highest instances of rape for a country not at war. We are an incredibly violent country and I would argue that much of this violence is as a result of men who fiercely seek to protect patriarchy and the social advantages that is bestowed to men.

Patriarchy is amazingly complex because it's like a massive hand that cradles men but simultaneously holds them in a vice grip. It not only dictates how women ought to act but also commands a kind of hyper-masculinity that is incompatible with tenderness or weakness. As much as men have violently sought to keep women in check, men also ridicule and humiliate men that show any vulnerability. You see this in the egregious homophobia some men show toward Gay men and the assumptions some make about the sexual orientations of many effeminate men.

Patriarchy is a unique social construct that transcends gender, sexuality, age and class. Its effects are oppressive and long lasting. Problems aren't solved by merely pointing them out, we need to have honest conversations in our homes and in public spaces about how to reconstruct the South African male architype. We need to create safe spaces for men to freely express themselves in ways that aren't self-destructive and that don't hurt those closest to them.

Peril Seven: It's A Man's World
| Felicia Thobejane

It's a man's world.

A phrase we hear too often.
But a phrase that holds true in today's society. Especially when you're a young womxn entrepreneur.

A man's world has major implications for womxn entrepreneurs.

As womxn we are expected to modify ourselves to be able to excel in an environment that won't make room for us. We are expected to try and sit at a table that wasn't even designed for us. We are expected to be slaying it in meetings whilst worrying if our outfit is trying too hard. Let's not even get to if you have natural hair and you get told that it looks unprofessional. But that's another peril for another day.

Essentially, everything in life is arranged to the advantage of men. As I understand Patriarchy to be defined as a system of society in which men hold the power and womxn are largely excluded from it.

Life is tough for women.

Life is even more taxing when you are a business womxn. *Excuse the pun.*

Entrepreneurship is largely patriarchal because womxn are generally undermined in the business world. As the definition indicates, the business world has never had a place for us, unless we were serving tea or cleaning up after the men had conducted with the day's dealings. I've been in rooms where my opinion didn't matter because of my gender, whereas if a man shared the same idea it would be applauded. I've been sexualized by male clients because womxn "aren't reputable business service providers".

Can you imagine that?

I grew up in a female-headed household where I was always encouraged to do my best and be whoever I wanted to be, no matter the kind of environment I was in. Thinking back to my childhood, perhaps not having a constant male figure around blinded me to the effects of how deeply patriarchy runs in society. I went to an all-girls high school, which also shielded me from patriarchy. As I got to university, my eyes were more opened, where the boys at the male residences were being trained to basically treat womxn like objects, but again, that's another peril for another day.

As a growing entrepreneur, there are days I find myself riddled with anxiety from the thought of interacting with my male counterparts. It is a vicious cycle that one can never really be mentally prepared for. As I never know whether to brace myself for possibly being objectified, or to brace myself for the murmurs of why I'm trying to fit into a man's world or to train myself for the conversations with men who constantly belittle me because of my gender. In my four years of being an entrepreneur, the strangest of things have happened where patriarchy has been more than evident. But the day it slapped me in the face was more recent than you'd think.

On the 29th of December 2019, someone I considered a close friend said, and I quote, "What did women do to help the human race besides give birth?
Everything on this planet a man made it. Medicine, technology, laws. Like seriously what did women do for the human race?"

Those words circle my brain more often than I'd like them to and they leave me with a bitter taste in my mouth every time. But those words always get me thinking about how often womxn are told they can't do certain jobs, especially in male-dominated industries. Then I think about the changes we're seeing happening across the globe surrounding gender equality in the workplace, and I ask myself whether womxn are being uplifted in those spaces purely for corporate governance or because womxn are just as skilled and capable as men?

These questions I ask myself about gender equality and the statements I hear about how useless womxn are remind me why I have chosen to build a womxn centred empire. Every day I am reminded, although painfully, why I wanted to make just one more thing easier for womxn starting up their businesses. I have come to realize that for a very long time, we are going to be fighting the war of patriarchy alone without the support of the men in our lives. I have come to realize that, as womxn, we're going to have to uplift one another until we're equal to our male counterparts. And as a business owner of a company that focuses predominantly on the development of womxn owned businesses, I face the challenge of men constantly telling me how sexist our mission is without truly understanding it, but you know what? That's ok. Remember my friend from earlier? I haven't spoken to him since then, which is probably a problem on my part for not doing better at educating him about the consequences of saying things like that about womxn. But I have a feeling that once he finds his quote in this book, he might start to understand the implications of words and actions aligned with the school of thought he has on the topic of womxn. *I think I'll send him a copy as an early birthday gift...*

I've been fighting the urge to send him a long list of womxn in history who have contributed to the existence of so many technologies and sciences because I'm afraid that in my pursuit, I might lash out at how myopic he is, but I decided to be better than that.

The patriarchy makes me angry. It makes me angry because of how it has conditioned us to think that womxn are not as important as men in society. It makes me angry that there are womxn so blinded by years of accepting it as a norm, that even they have become perpetrators in the process.

It makes me angry that womxn have to carry the burden of overcoming a system that was designed to oppress them and make them seem inferior, when in fact they are the strong ones. How long do we have to carry the weight of the world on our shoulders before we are heard? How many more marches against gender-based violence do we need to endure? How many more petitions for equal pay do we need to sign? How many more womxn-headed households need to keep surviving until the ball is finally in our court? The answer should be zero, but that would mean that I would be living in a utopia.

The patriarchy makes me angry. I had to remind myself to breathe quite a few times while writing this because I didn't realise just how many of my frustrations were bottled up. I didn't realize how tired I was of fighting a seemingly never-ending war, tired of justifying why womxn are just as good as men and that we're not asking to be given the upper-hand, but rather to be treated like humans just as men are. It feels like we're always being taught a lesson, but I'm not quite sure what the lesson is other than how to endure more pain. And believe it or not, it's the smallest things that lead to an accumulation of frustration. It's asking a womxn if her new hair was sponsored by a "girlfriend allowance", it's the fragile masculinity attached to being intimidated by a womxn who drives a big car or has a bold voice, it's the assumption that a womxn cannot be successful without the influence of a man in her life. All of these things, both big and small, are the reason we walk around carrying so much fear and frustration.

It still makes me angry that men always feel attacked by the sheer mention of the word: Feminism. Let me just clarify that Feminism is not attacking men. It is attacking the Patriarchy. If we could keep the true definition of Feminism, (that is the advocacy of womxn's rights on the ground of the equality of the sexes) at the core of our values and ideals at all times - it would be so much easier to treat each human being with fairness and kindness. Note that I said human beings and not just womxn. We all deserve to be given a chance to live our lives without fearing if we'll even make it back home. We all deserve the access to the same opportunities and we all deserve to be given a voice to speak on the issues that we're passionate about.

I am so fortunate to be surrounded more often than not, by people who are not blinded to the long term effects of how womxn have suffered the wrath of being inferior to a man.

Powerhouses, like the other authors in this book, constantly remind me why it's so important to use our voices every chance we're given. It's always enlightening when I hear people, especially men, asking how they can be a part of dismantling patriarchy and these are the conversations we should be driving amongst each other to consciously make an effort at understanding the effects of our actions and the words we speak.

It's not easy trying to fight and dismantle a social system that impacts and affects us in different settings. It's a vicious cycle, but it can be broken. If we make it clear that womxn can, and should, make their voices be heard, we can upend the gender imbalances that exist across numerous male-dominated fields. If we make it clear, that womxn can hold executive business positions with their own choice of being able to be nurturers, caretakers, and providers at home, then we can upend the gender imbalance. If we make it clear, from a very young age, that calling young girls bossy - in fact does not mean that they are too annoying, too emotional and too controlling to run their own businesses and companies, then we can possibly upend gender imbalances in our society. If we make it clear that womxn are capable of achieving absolutely anything they put their minds to, then patriarchy can possibly be a thing of the past.

Peril Eight: Who Really Runs the World?

| Cassandra Moodley

Part 1. Leadership

I once read a tweet – and really, I'm paraphrasing here – about how boys are told from an early age that one day, they will be the "man of the house" (a position synonymous with leadership and authority), while girls are trained from an early age to actually lead a household. Strange, isn't it?

My observation, fairly unbiased and subject to review, is that gender dictates leadership, not quality. And while that's hardly an earth-shattering revelation, I constantly find it disturbing that the status quo, for the most part, remains intact. In this section, I want to examine why this is the case; this is not an attack on men nor their leadership abilities en masse, instead this is a reflection on how society functions to maintain outdated gender norms, and how it can have a perverse effect on men and women alike.

I personally represent a few intersections being black, adopted into an Indian family and privy to white culture as the dominant society I grew up in. There are plenty cultural and religious practices that scream of patriarchy in that upbringing alone. But I'm more intrigued by how, as a society, we've made leaps and bounds in many aspects, and yet we're still seeing gatekeeper tendencies from both men and women.

So, in a post-modern society, where for the most part, people live outside of religious and cultural bounds, how does this idea of gendered leadership prevail? I think that (badly paraphrased) tweet is a clue. I remember a story I was told about how when I was a baby, my dad had a medical emergency and was rushed to hospital in the middle of the night. My brother, five years my senior, solemnly declared to my mom that he was now "the man of the house". He must've been about seven or eight. What he meant, was that he was the sole male and assumed the role of protector, but what he unknowingly implied in that statement, was that at seven or eight, by virtue of his gender, he was next in line for leadership. I wonder what sort of impact that has on a child? This idea that by birth you are to assume important areas of leadership, graduate to adulthood whether you're prepared or not. I wonder what kind of stressors come with being the "man of the house", at any age, and if this conferred responsibility corresponds with the distressing rates of male suicide?

When you think you are the "man of the house" – what does that really mean? Does that mean you cannot show fear and anxiety in the face of danger and uncertainty? Does it mean that your role is that of father, brother, uncle, security guard, financial aid, sole decision maker? And concerns in these areas are to be borne by one person and one person alone? Time and time again we see that families function better when responsibilities are shared and decision making is inclusive and consultative. There should never be a need for a seven or eight-year-old to think he has graduated into adulthood based on his gender. Husbands and wives, in my opinion, enter into a partnership; and increasingly this has become one where men need to step into traditionally female roles and vice versa.

Leading a household requires a number of skills: good finance, maintenance, emotional and physical wellbeing of the family unit, cleaning, cooking, design. I think we need to do away with the proverbial "man of the house" and start looking at families and households as a whole unit, that works best with the combined efforts of all parties. The next area one might encounter gendered leadership is in school. High school in particular, is an interesting microcosm for some of the real world examples of how gendered leadership often sells men short.

Now, while I cannot speak for all high schools, I can certainly attest to the many co-ed and single sex high schools in the greater Durban area. The criteria, it seems, for Head Boy boils down to one thing: sport. Now, while there's absolutely nothing wrong with achieving on the field, this is in stark comparison to the Head Girl position, which require female leads to be all round achievers in academics, culture/sport and general leadership ability. I've heard the argument that being appointed as the captain of a sport, in a male context, is leadership in itself, and I don't dispute that. This argument has also been substantiated many times by the "fact" that any young man who has attained the confidence of his peers by proving himself on the field, is someone with leadership qualities that extend beyond sport, to applying the same grit, determination, sportsmanship and charisma to the rest of the school environment.

If that's you right now, let me tell you, I hear you.

My point here is, the same just isn't true for women and girls. As with most things in life, it is required that we go above and beyond to prove our leadership ability and not just in one area, but several. One of the best Head Girls I've ever had the bliss of learning under, was the epitome of leadership and success. A straight A student, captain of the debating team (with SA colours), participated annually in the midmar mile, demonstrated leadership in the Representative Council of Learners every year. She achieved honours in academics, leadership and culture and was the third person in the history of my school to ever earn a white blazer, and to top it all off, HILARIOUS, good-natured and approachable. Her counterpart at our brother school in the same year? Captained hockey.

Why do we tell men that they don't have to be multitalented and exceptional, yet demand this from women as an entry level? Again, women are just as much gatekeepers as men in this regard. To our benefit, this makes us far more adjusted individuals that are able to continue pushing the boundaries to achieve, but to our detriment, if we don't, we're automatically disqualified. This is where I wonder if women, particularly women of colour's Imposter Syndrome comes from? This undeniable belief that we're never doing enough to prove we're worth the accolades we achieve, even when we're already operating past capacity. I'm in no way suggesting men, and again particularly men of colour, don't experience Imposter Syndrome, but I know from personal experience that every woman I know has experienced or regularly experiences feelings of inadequacies, despite being literal superheroes, changing the landscape of this country in various ways.

These inequalities in how we view capacity and ability to lead don't just stop in high school. They follow us and find themselves nicely entrenched in the workplace. Which leads me to my next area of reflection. I remember having an interesting chat with my significant other. While he was working in the corporate banking sector, his line manager – a woman – questioned why there were more female graduates in post-graduate degrees than males, yet the same was not true in terms of senior management and leadership.

Now, while I'm the first to agree that ability to lead doesn't boil down to academics alone, it got me thinking that it cannot be possible that the vast majority of women with postgraduate knowledge of their areas of expertise, in a wide range of career paths, simply don't have the ability to lead.

The math just doesn't add up.

It cannot be, that the vast majority of women who are passionate, educated and experienced in the ICT, finance, engineering, medical fields etc. lack leadership qualities. Worse still, I feel women are not just excluded from positions of leadership, they are often sabotaged. When KPMG was going through its worst crisis, the all-male leadership team was let go with severance packages, faced little to no public scrutiny and distanced themselves from the mess they had caused. Interestingly, KPMG suddenly hired their first ever black, female CEO - in over 100 years of existence. Ms Nhlamulo Dlomu faced the full scourge of public scrutiny, attempting the impossible task of saving the company's tarnished reputation. If this is what we label transformation in the private sector of South Africa, believe me, we don't want it!

Perhaps the grossest injustice in recent history, is former CEO of the South African Institution of Civil Engineering (SAICE), Manglin Pillay's July 2018 article, "Out on a Rib". As we know, engineering is an already male-dominated career path, with plenty horror stories from women who choose this field, from unresolved sexual harassment cases to hostile work environments. The fact that women face difficulty in this field and its disciplines, has little to do with their academic capabilities and much to do with gender. Back to Misogynist Manglin – his article in the SAICE magazine questioned the efforts being made to attract and retain female talent in the fields of STEM (science, technology, engineering and maths) because, according to Mr Pillay, women are "better suited to people or caring industries". Further, Mr Pillay had mansplained that women busy themselves with "more important enterprises like, family and raising children, than to be at the beck and call off shareholders".

The domino effect of teaching little boys that they have little to do in order to earn positions of leadership seemingly creates an alternate reality where the contributions of women are overlooked, undermined and dismissed. Boys learn that they only need be good at one thing to be considered as leaders, while their female counterparts exhaust themselves doing twice as much, to be seen as half as good. This system of gendered leadership is what allowed SAICE to originally accept Mr Pillay's written apology (which was regurgitated PR) citing his "contribution to the civil engineering industry", prior to his eventual dismissal. This is an example of what happens when we don't hold leaders, regardless of gender, to a higher standard. Mr Pillay did not need to have a high EQ, in order to be nominated CEO. Mr Pillay did not have to have an understanding of interpersonal relations, to be appointed CEO. Mr Pillay was not required to prove leadership qualities beyond application of his work, to earn the title of CEO. All the while, Mr Pillay, with his antiquated views, would've undoubtedly held back talented women with proven track records of excellence in multiple areas of life, work and leadership because of his personal views. How do we know this? Because Mr Pillay's article, "Out on a Rib", went through an editing process, and was still submitted for publication – which means no one at SAICE thought anything was wrong with that article. And that, in my opinion, is the problem with gendered leadership.

Part 2. The Workplace

I've had the pleasure of working in numerous environments - informally, formally, casually, permanently – you name it, I've done it (even a silent art auction). My experiences have given me a glimpse into how the workplace can be a wildly different in terms of experience, based on gender. Working any customer service job gives you an insight into the human condition and allows you to understand how power dynamics come into play just about all day! I managed a restaurant for about two and a half years, and that experience was truly enlightening. The first difference I noticed between my male and female staff was how easily men could blur the lines of professionalism and friendliness, without fear of misconstrued intentions. One of the biggest complaints I would receive from customers was related to a lot of my female staff members and their "attitudes" – they didn't smile as much, chat as much or engage as much. Following up on complaints almost always lead to counter-complaints; this customer had gotten tipsy during her last shift and made her feel uncomfortable; the next customer had taken her friendliness for flirting and won't stop asking for her number. One of the worst days was watching video footage of a 60-something year old regular customer, follow a visibly upset waitress into the restaurant, and smack her across the bum. I had never dealt with a single complaint of that nature with any of the male staff.

Sexual harassment aside, it is difficult being female in the workplace. I could write an academic thesis on being interrupted during meetings, being ignored during presentations and generally dealing with double standards. Perhaps the root of all workplace evil is the patriarchal culture that exists in large corporations, commonly known as the 'Boys Club'.

To most men's credit, I don't even think they know when and how the Boys Club forms, but the camaraderie they experience socially, often interplays into professionalism. I remember having a conversation with a close male friend about his new senior manager, at a leading banking institution. His firs remark was that she looked annoying; a woman who hadn't so much as clocked in a full day's work yet. Now I'm not saying first impressions don't count, only that it's interesting to note the kind of adjectives ascribed to female leadership by men. Fast forward a few weeks, and it would appear that the initial idea of annoyance was confirmed, and justified by the fact that this woman wanted to do everything "by the book". It didn't at all occur that perhaps as a new employee, and of very few female senior managers, she was trying to do her job the right way, or that she would be judged more harshly for any mistakes she would make. Worse, women seem to represent the collective, so the mistakes of one female senior leader, is a mistake on behalf of female leaders everywhere. What really intrigued me, is how it was explained that prior to this lady coming in, the position was filled by a man, who knew the guys on his floor personally and would approve their work without much oversight on his behalf. Which is why he lost his job, but apparently that made him "cool". This Boys Club exists and it's a network that works to exclude women; perhaps not intentionally, but the systemic devaluation of women in leadership positions, that men reinforce, are ignored – making room for further justification of the Boys Club mentality.

Part 3. Male Dominated Industries

Now I know I've touched on this a bit under leadership, but this bears unpacking on its own. My approach here is to help some men who've maybe never considered what women in their industry go through, and highlight some tangible ways they can be allies. The tricky part of male dominated industries is that patriarchal practices are entrenched in the culture of the job, making it an uphill battle for women to enter and remain in certain fields of practice. The lack of women in senior positions leaves a gaping hole for mentorship, and often women fall through the cracks, either in an academic setting or in the workplace.

What is it about the presence of women that so greatly disturbs men? Until maybe six to ten years ago, women broadcasting in sport was a point of contention for a lot of South African men. The outrage, completely unmatched to the perceived "crime" centred around misinformed ideas that women knew nothing about sport, and would ruin the delivery of pre and post-match content. There is an ease with which men assume women are incompetent, and this certainly echoes through the ways in which men interact with women in the workplace.

A few years ago, an American workplace experiment took place which revealed the gender bias that exists within the professional working environment. Two sales people swapped emails, and exposed themselves to differences in communication the other party received. The man in this scenario was a top-earning salesman and was able to close deals in the space of a week, while the lady straggled behind, unable to successfully convince as many buyers, or solve queries as quickly. Following the email swap, the man realized that nearly every single query he attempted to resolve was second-guessed and met with doubt, while the lady had the best week of her life; making record sales and solving queries simply and easily. There exists, in the minds of both women and men, a gendered bias that men are more capable than women. This is something I strongly feel we all need to check ourselves on. One of the biggest issues with male dominated industries is that harmful practices and toxic work culture often go unchecked. Sorry to pick on mining once again, but I had a friend go through the induction process at one of the big mining companies in South Africa. Her excited surprise to see a female leading at least in one area (HR), quickly turned to dismay; the induction included a list of clothes women should not wear in order to avoid unwanted male attention. They were being reminded that the status quo exists; men should not go out of their way to be respectful, women should expect that men will harass them, and were thus given survival tips to avoid this. At their place of work. This also means that if any woman were to go to HR to report sexual harassment, she would likely first be questioned on what she was wearing. This is unfortunately not the only example; another close friend in the field of auditing was told by another, senior woman, that she should consider dying her hair, as her natural blonde colour doesn't inspire confidence in her intellect, and that she herself has had greater success as a brunette. It is amazing how the "innocent jokes" we grew up with seem to come to life as soon as we leave the bubble of university.

My last thought on male dominated industries is how a lot of men who actually work alongside females in these industries are quietly supportive. They're not harassers, they don't undermine a woman's intelligence and they certainly create space. However, quiet support is not what is needed. When men like Manglin Pillay make outlandish and sexist remarks, we need our quiet supporters to speak up. When men start commenting and rating the incoming young female interns (an appallingly common phenomenon and work place practice in big corporates) we need our quiet supporters to call it out. Most importantly, when women show unease around a fellow co-worker, we need our quiet supporters to believe us. All too often, there are power dynamics at play that make navigating the workplace a minefield for women. Sexual harassment is covert; it's a look, an ambiguous comment said in the right tone to convey meaning while the words themselves seem innocent, it's the accidental slip of a hand and far too many women feeling they need to remain silent.

I know I said I was done, but one last thing okay? Let's celebrate each other! I am yet to come across a woman in a female dominated industry bash a man for choosing that career path, or accuse him of being a gender quota taking a job he hasn't rightfully earned. No, I see women supporting hairstylists, male and female. I see women supporting chefs, male and female. I see women grateful for nurses, male and female. I know men are grateful for our presence – we just need a little more support.

Conclusion:

My original chapter was never meant to cover gender-based violence, but at the time of writing this, the dust has just begun to settle on this issue after the horrible death of Uyinene.

My brothers, I am talking directly to you. Feminism has never been more relevant than right now, and we need you, each and every one of you, to understand what feminism is, and what it is not. When this country was reeling from the deaths of so many – too many – beautiful young women, at the hands of men they didn't know as well as men they loved, that was feminism in action. In fact, it is a direct response to the oppression we face at the hands of our counterparts.

Someone once asked on Twitter, "Ladies, what would you do if men had a curfew at 21h00." The responses were so innocently heart-breaking – go for a walk, go for a run at night in Summer, go out for a drink without worrying what would happen travelling alone late at night. These are things we still do, but knowing full well we're potentially putting our lives at risk. And the thing is, we don't want to live in a world without men! We loved you, we appreciate you, we have fun with you, we want to dance with you and chat to you and get to know you.

The sad reality is Karabo Mokoena tried to leave an abusive relationship, and she ended up dead, her body burnt and left in a ditch.
The sad reality is Siam Lee was pursued by a man obsessed with her, and she ended up dead; her body burnt and left in a field.

The sad reality is Leighandre "Baby Lee" Jegels was a professional boxer, more than capable of defending herself, was shot dead by her boyfriend.

The sad reality is:

- Priska Schalk.
- Anene Booysen.
- Popi Qwabe.
- Bongeka Phungula.
- Hannah Cornelius.
- Lethukuthula Ngobese.

Peril Nine: A Feminist Orgasm
| Milvia Iannantouni

This chapter is about sex.

This chapter is about dating.

This chapter is about harassment.

This chapter is a private narrative of my life that goes public.

A note to whoever is reading this chapter for the wrong reasons:

If you are about to use what is written in this chapter to judge me, shame me and try to "ruin" my career/life, I'm sorry for you, because the things you want to use to destroy me are the same ones who prove that you are a sexist human being.

I thought about what to write in this chapter for a long period of time; I wanted it to be a true representation of myself, I wanted it to help my healing and help you understand. I'm Milvia, I'm 22 years old when writing this chapter, and I'm on the journey of loving my body, pleasing myself and living my sexuality without constraints. This chapter will tell you very private stories of my life and hopefully will show you the consequences that the hegemonic vision of femininity and of our sexuality has on my daily life.

I was *swiping* on Tinder when I finally realized that the subject of this chapter should be about sex and dating, about living my sexuality under the patriarchy and the constraints and limits that it imposes on me. It wasn't easy to convince myself to write this chapter, I was and still am afraid of the repercussions that talking freely about sex and dating will cause to my future self. But I'm also aware that I'm not alone, that I'm not the only womxn who feels this way, who struggles with their sexual life because of the society we live in. I'm not the only one who is harassed, and I'm definitely not the only one scared about the future and the judgment of people.

But if not now, when? When will we tell the untellable, get rid of the taboos that society has pushed on us since we were born and talk about the problems of our generation? If not me, who? Voicing those problems is the first step to solve them and hope that the future generation will have a healthy relation to their bodies, sex and sexuality. I'm still scared, I'm still thinking about the consequences of this chapter on my future life, but I'm happy to take those risks if only one womxn will feel less sorry and ashamed about their sexuality after reading this chapter. Also, it is important for me to state that what is said in this chapter by no means represents the experience of every womxn. I'm a white, European, cis-gender woman, queer, with a middle-class background and I'm very aware of the privileges that come with some of my identities and I'm by no means trying to represent any other womxn than me. What I'm trying to do is to voice my own experiences, in the hope that others will share their own experiences and have a broader vision of what it means to experience the peril of patriarchy.

I understand patriarchy as a system of oppression that goes beyond the willingness of every single individual involved in it. It is a social, economic, cultural and political construction that influences us at every level of our society. It affects everyone, no one is exempt from it, but it affects everyone differently and every one of us is part of it. We cooperate in reproducing this system, sometimes consciously and sometimes not. I have committed the crime of perpetuating the system ever since I was born, and the first step to change is admitting to being part of this problem and try to get rid of the dogma that this system imposes on us. One of the implications of the system we face is having to answer these questions on a daily basis:

What does it mean to be a womxn in this world?

What are the constraints imposed on us and which ones do we impose on ourselves without knowing?

What is being a good woman? Is there such a thing?

Do we have to aspire to be the woman that society wants us to be? Or should we be our own selves and try to break that cocoon, that chrysalis and fly away?

Femininity can be defined in so many different ways, but today I want you to think about the manner in which society wants us to be. How many times have you heard womxn being slut-shamed? Or you have done it to someone? I have slut-shamed in the past and it has also happened to me. Because in this system we are both the victim and the perpetrator. The society portrays us and our sexuality as fragile gems to protect. The weight that has been put on our virginity is just one of the most flagrant examples of this vision society has. Female pleasure is almost unspoken.

Clitoris, G-spot, orgasm, porn, erotica, masturbation: those are words we shall not say. And when we say them we become "easy", we lose our purity status and we deserve anything that will then happen to us.

I want to testify this with a story. If you know me, you have probably already heard about this, and if you were there that day you probably know how hard it is for me to speak about it and how ashamed and dirty I felt. This is just a normal story of harassment. Isn't it sad? We, womxn, use the word "normal" to describe harassment because it is so widespread and regular to hear about it that we expect it to happen.

This is what I wrote that night.

20th April 2019, Johannesburg

Tonight, the patriarchy knocked at my window and it was harder than what I could have imagined. This man that used to live at the residence, which I thought was still living there, came to my window (I live at the garden level) and knocked at 9 o'clock pm.

I opened it because he was not moving from my window. He first told me that I have been rude to him because I used to never say hi to him on a daily basis.

Then, he went on asking me if he could enter to chat. I

declined. I am studying, I said. He kept on asking me to enter and then asked me to then exit and smoke a cigarette together.

At this point, I was already pissed off and could not close the window because he had put his head in the middle. I tried to close the conversion. He said he would have leave after asking me a question. I said to go on because the only thing I wanted was him to leave.

"I see you have lubricant in your room, What do you use it for? Sex? Anal? Don't be shy. The first time I used it, it was for anal sex."

"I use it for sex", I said, trying to make him go away. "With or without condoms?" He then asked.

I answered because I felt there was no way of getting out of this.

My door on the other side was open and I started feeling tense and wanted to answer his questions as fast as possible to get rid of him.

"Oh, so you have condoms in your room? Can I see them? Which one do you use?

"No, I'm not going to show you my condoms." I was shocked by the shamelessness he had.

"Can I ask you the last question and then I promise I'll leave?". "Would you fuck me?". I froze, he had his hands on my window, my door was not closed, there was a party outside, no one would have heard if something had to happen.

"NO."

"Why not? Maybe I should come back and ask you tomorrow, today is not our day"

"NO."

```
He left, I ran to close my
door.
```

That night I realized it. The condoms and lubricant in my room, for me they were a sign of a healthy and safe relationship with my sexual life, but for that man, they were the visual proof of my availability. The unspoken confession of my desire to have sex with men and therefore, with him. Because I could not live my sexuality without living it with every man. I was "easy", I was supposedly attracted by the very essence of a man, no matter if I liked him or not. This was his vision of me. If I liked sex enough to not have to hide my condoms and lubricant, then, having sex with him should not have been a problem. I then realized that I have been to the room of many male friends, their condoms were just lying everywhere, and it was no problem. But when I went to the security and told this story, the woman at the security told me: "Ok, I will take notice of the accident, but for the future notice you should probably hide your condoms, it gives the wrong message to men."

My freedom gave the wrong message to men.

My body gave the wrong message to men.

A skirt, a smile, a condom, words, movements, clothes, breathing…

Are we supposed to calculate every single thing in our lives to not give wrong messages to men?

The only message I would love men to understand is: **my freedom does not imply your freedom on my body**.

We have been taught to be scared, to act a certain way and to understand the dangers around us. We have been brought up by people telling us to always keep an eye open, to have fun but not too much, to be aware of who is around, not to dress in a certain way, to be and not to be at the same time. Our sisters, mothers, and aunts have spent all their energies to ensure our safety and teach us how to be safe in this society, but no one ever thought them anything. Imbalance of effort into making sure they won't become what makes us feel unsafe. No one wants to see their sons, brothers, uncles and dads as part of the problem, the aggressor, the cat-caller, the rapist, the abuser, the bad guy, is always the "other". But this "other" is the son of someone, and more than anything, he is the son of our society.

But as daughters and sons, as children of this society, we can act. Our lives can be the proof of our society changing. I'm not saying it is easy, I'm not saying you have to do it, but that is what I think about all the time. I could be living my life conforming to the norms our society gave me, listening and following carefully the commands of my mother, as many daughters have been doing, but I'm not. I want us to talk about sex, sexuality, love, passion, dating, pleasure and self-acceptance. I want us to explore my life together and together see the hurtful impacts of the patriarchy. I've been raised to believe virginity was something to be protected, keep it for yourself, it is the proof of your love for yourself and your value. I thought this was the reality, till the time I realized that dealing with my pleasure and my needs was the best way to love myself and value myself. I never used to talk about masturbation, men do masturbate, it is normal for them, but not for us, right? We don't talk about it, we don't share it with one another when we are younger, we have a distorted relationship with pleasure because we don't talk about it. Our pleasure is unspoken, our stories' secrets and our relationship with our own bodies closeted.

How can we be growing up to change the preconceptions our society has on us if we don't even fully know what we are talking about. I spent the last three years rediscovering my body, my pleasure, myself. The judgments of others, of my family, my friends, has not been easy to deal with. I've been crucified by many, many men mainly but also womxn of all generations.

I've been called a slut for not saying sorry about my sexual life. One-night standing is a "man thing" apparently. But I would assume straight men do not engage in one night standing alone. How could it be that they are the only ones allowed to those sexual experiences? The womxn sleeping with them is always faulty, incorrect, doing wrong, but not them. She becomes easy, they are normal. This is the double standard of our society. We are not allowed to explore and experiment, we are not men. In the last years, I've tried to be different, to exist outside of this double standard. I've tried to not feel the judgment of the people around me, to rightfully do what I wanted to do without the need of the society consenting to it. People said, "I've been sleeping around", I prefer saying I've been having different sexual partners, all consenting to engage in non-committal sexual relations. I am still very surprised by how much people feel the need to know about my sexual life, but I've come to live with it. If you want to know, I'll tell you, because I hope the way I talk about it will be some sort of education for you, either by teaching you to respect my choices or helping you allowing yourself to live freely. But, there have been times when I felt this society was coming for me, when I felt the judgment and for a second, thought about giving up.

We are the product of years of fear, of years of conditioning upon our existence and it is almost impossible to free ourselves from all that pressure put on us. Using dating apps, finding one night stand, it always comes with stress, waiting for someone you don't know at the entrance of a bar, always triggers me, reminds me of my "condition", my "womxnhood". No matter if the man I'm about to see turns out to be a "normal guy", that fear that comes with the fragility and powerless of my existence is always haunting my thoughts.

And I want to be clear, we, womxn, are by no means weak, our essence is not, but society has taught us to be weak. Think about your youth, you as a child… Your existence has been defined by your gender, you were a little girl and therefore you needed to act a certain way. It is not a surprise that many womxn find themselves powerless in situations of aggression, domination, harassment, we have been nurtured to be fragile and weak. Many are the womxn today fighting against this status quo, and many have done it in the past, but we cannot deny the fear that this condition brings to our existence, to our survival.

Acknowledging our angst, does not mean accepting the status quo, it means recognising the roots of the patriarchal system. Because our anxiety, our fear, our weakness, those characteristics define our role in the system. I've been scared, I've been afraid of living my sexuality freely and I still am. The angst won't fade away the moment you take back control of your sexuality, but you will learn to cope with that feeling, to find a balance to have a healthy relationship with yourself in a world that is not made for you. Many were the times I realised the society in which I was living (and I've lived in four completely different countries - Ivory Coast, Italy, France, South Africa) wasn't made for my existence, I could survive, sure, but I could not be me. My sexual existence was not meant to be, my way of speaking about pleasure was not supposed to be spoken. My understanding of womxnhood completely inopportune for the standards on which this society was running. And this came with many misunderstandings and misconceptions about my choices and my life.

Last summer on a night-out with some friends, I was "pimped" by one of my male friends. He decided that since I was talking openly about my sexual life, that had to mean that I was ready to have sex with anyone. Therefore, he told one of his friends, which I met that night and didn't talk to, that I would have slept with him. Of course, this didn't happen. I made it clear that he was one man that I would not have done it with, because I was not attracted by him and I just didn't want to.

At the moment I had a strong delusional feeling toward my friend, because it seemed to me like he had completely misunderstood my life and my choices. But the delusion came to become angst and fear. Again, I was facing a reality I could not escape: men understand freedom as their freedom over my body. And even if that story didn't end up with any harassment or aggression, the thinking-process behind their actions could have led to that. And please, again, my fear is not my defeat, it is just part of this learning process and I'm willing to be scared if it means that I'm trying to change the status quo. Changing the status quo, that is the aim for the future of our societies, but how?

I do not believe I'm in the place to give anyone a comprehensive approach to a global reality with different facet's in different countries and intersections with many other types of discrimination. But I believe our experiences, if voiced, can impact change. Loud womxn saying uncomfortable realities to the world, this is what I hope for the future. Womxn investing into the education of younger generations because this patriarchal culture has to be changed from its roots. I want sexual education to be thought, I want us to be able to decide over our own bodies and sexualities, and I want men to understand my freedom as my own business.

But how? I don't think there is an easy solution for such a complex problem, what I do know is that I'll keep on being loud about my own pleasure and hope if we all talk about our own experiences this may start our own sexual revolution and the fall of the patriarchy.

Peril Ten: All Rights Reserved to Him

|Thuli Nduvane

My journey with the shadow of patriarchy has been a dark one. The memories come flooding back, quickly and in abundance. Which one to write about first is the bigger question?

We have met so many times. Many of those times to my detriment, some (I'm ashamed to admit) weren't as unpleasant because they served me or gave me a "pass". Sometimes the residue of the shadow sticks on you like how thick cigarette smoke sticks to your favorite jacket after a night out. Now you smell like it. Sometimes it seeps into your skin and becomes a part of you and reveals itself when you open your mouth. It contaminates your thoughts, opinions, perceptions and interactions, many times (for me) unknowingly.

In my time on these streets, I've taken some notes, learnt some lessons and have found various ways to finesse the system in a way that keeps me alive and safe and these days, that is the greatest win to walk away with. I have recently become the kind of woman who rates all my Uber drivers five stars, purely because they didn't abduct and kill me.

That's the only standard I have.

Forget the fact that the car seats are stained and gross and smell like feet and cigarettes. "You get five stars, sir! Thank you for not kidnapping me and making me a statistic!" I've only recently started engaging with the world as a game that women constantly need to navigate through a set of rules. I recently co-wrote and devised a play with exceptional women that happen to be great friends of mine as well as my colleagues; Aalliyah Matintela and Sibahle Mangena. *Text Me When You Arrive* has taught me that life, particularly for women, is tricky and if you don't abide by the dehumanizing rules: You might just become a statistic.

Each rule is more ridiculous than the next. Each rule is more degrading than the next. Each rule is more uncomfortable than the next. Each rule is more bizarre than the next. But for some reason, we continue to make negotiations with these wild situations and it just becomes about getting out alive and unharmed. Because of this we just go with it, no matter how much of our dignity we lose in the middle of it. These rules guide us on the path to avoiding becoming another heart-breaking headline. They "protect" us and "ensure" that we make it home and hopefully live to see another day. Some of these rules are explored in the play *Text Me When You Arrive*, some are from my personal archive of life lessons. Like many of us, I encountered my first lessons at home, from observation and learnt behavior. You don't realize that your body is absorbing all of this information that will one day equip you to "defend" yourself against the perils of patriarchy.

Girl child, do not ask questions!
The earliest lesson that quickly became a fundamental rule as a girl child occurred while having my precious teacher-teacher play time cut short. Mind you, I took this time extremely seriously, because your girl was always a bad-ass

teacher and I'd waited all week for it to finally be my turn to boss everyone around! Being told to come inside to wash the dishes (that my boy cousin and I had dirtied together) was just the beginning of my eyes being opened to a reality that was chosen for me. I was called inside while Junior was left in peace to play marbles with the boys. I remember feeling angry, like this was unfair. Today I realize that that feeling was the first time I "feminized" (or whatever the doing word is for feminism) I met feminism and patriarchy all at once. I fought, questioned, argued, huffed and puffed my way to a beating. I guess this was when I learnt that the first rule to navigating this space as a girl was to never ever question my grandparents about anything, much less what my role was under their roof, or what I could or couldn't do "as a girl".

I'll be completely honest. I really didn't learn the first time. I definitely continued to question and got my bums handed to me, time and time again. Today, at my big age I know better. Do not think for yourself (out loud, that is!). Do not ask why you have to wash the dishes, cook, clean and be home a certain time. Just obey the rules, because running the risk of being known as a "straat meisie" or "lazy" is the most dishonorable thing to be. A self-respecting, inquisitive queen has no space in the black family. Keep those questions and eye-rolls for your friends during teacher-teacher time.

Young Queen, take your home training seriously!

The concept of serving our fathers as some sort of "rehearsal" for serving your husband, hopefully, one day has always been the bedrock of the black, nuclear family. The words "your father is home!" were always meant to activate the starter wife/servant mode in us to get the kettle going for the tea/coffee, the plates must start making noise because Tata must be fed. You didn't choose his man or this life but all of a sudden, it has become your duty to serve and be a stand in. You better honour the opportunity to learn and get the best on-the-job training before you hit the big leagues.

Take your training days seriously my friend. This is your initiation school.

The Great Wall of Fake Name!

When creating the play; *Text Me When You Arrive* and even just thinking about these rules at the top of any South African woman's mind is making sure your fake name is at the ready, at the top of your head. No hesitation. No stuttering. Mine is Mbali. Don't ask me why. I really think I could look like a Mbali. Never mind the fact that I am clearly Xhosa and the name Mbali is very Zulu. I always manage to seamlessly avoid the Zulu conversation after dropping the Mbali-bomb. I don't really know why we should always have fake names at the ready. Maybe it just feels too close to our souls that the man on the street or the taxi driver knows our real names. Maybe we imagine that these men have some secret database that they can easily type up our names and find everything about us so we find some sort of safety in these aliases. These names become our armor and many times the only defense we have in the wilderness of the streets.

You exist for the male-gaze!

Does ignoring men on the streets and acting like they don't exist even constitute as a rule? I think I've come to accept that it is a natural instinct for every woman, not just the evolved and woke woman of today. I remember seeing my Mom do this as a kid. "Mom, I think that man is talking to you! Mom!"- babes wouldn't even flinch. She kept it moving like the man shouting "Baby! How are you?" wasn't even a concept. So even if this rule doesn't help keep you alive, it surely will save your time. Hand in hand with this rule is the room you must allow men to stare at you like you live and breathe for their eyes and admiration. I can only hope that one day I will be the type of woman who is brave enough to ask "WHAT ARE YOU LOOKING AT? YOU'RE MAKING ME UNCOMFORTABLE!" but right now, today, even as I write this, I will sit and endure the curious, rapey gaze of the waiters behind the counter. Periodically making awkward eye-contact with them, as they look away immediately because "Oh! I just caught you being creepy! " and in no time, the cycle continues. Don't fight it ladies. Let them stare at you, sexualize you and drool over you. We were made for them, right? Purely for their gaze and adoration. So work it Queen! For him and only him.

Leave your Feminism & stank face outside the taxi rank.

This one wasn't even a rule I taught myself! I recently was humbled by life and lost my car and therefore; my privilege to privacy and God-given right to not listen to Maskandi music on the radio every day. That long winded sentence basically means that my car broke down and never came back to life. Like any other resourceful black child, I realized I can't sit at home and moan about not having a car, so your girl learnt the ropes and started taking taxis (for the first time in my life). On one of these anxiety-filled first days of my new public transport journey, I'm walking through Bree taxi-rank. Neutral faced, of course, no one is walking through a taxi rank looking like the Joker. One of the drivers stops me, dead in my tracks and says (directly translated) with a smile on his face; "You're not going to walk around here looking so sure of yourself. Drop that attitude in your face when you're here. Not here, Sisi." Of course I was terrified about what would come after this 'gentle warning'. But he let me go on my merry way. I sat and reflected on this on the taxi. I chuckled out loud because, what a bizarre thing to say. You think you're keeping the peace just walking through life, trying to find your taxi, minding your business but little do you know, you're raging a war with your eyes, you're setting taxi ranks on fire with your Feminist aura. Ya, don't do that! Not in this South Africa and definitely not in this social climate. Leave your stank-face outside!

Ubers: The new mobile confession booths
With all the horror stories we hear about the dangers of taking Ubers, Taxify/ Bolts. I think we all enter these rides with caution, watching carefully that they proceed to the highlighted route and do not veer off of it, we send our loved ones our locations, we do the fake phone calls,

acting like you're telling your fake boyfriend that you are on your way in a white Toyota Corolla, with the registration plate you "sent him" knowing very well you don't have airtime, let alone a "big, scary, buff boyfriend" (or a boyfriend at all for that matter). After doing all of this, I can put money on the fact that none of us have been able to successfully avoid the 21 questions or confession session sitting at the back of the car. "So is the address I picked you up from where you live?" "Who do you live with?" "Where are you going?" "Who are you going to see?" "Oh... was that your boyfriend on the phone?" "What are you doing tonight?" "Eish, yaz... you should give me your number so you can show me around your area." "I'll come back and pick you up later on, if you don't mind."

The list of inappropriately invasive questions, suggestions and advances go on and on. We sit there delivering well-rehearsed lines and hope and pray all the traffic-lights are green and you can arrive at your destination as soon as possible, before he takes one wrong turn that you cannot come back from. He is entitled to this information. You owe him your life story, Sis. ID number, place of birth, tax number, place of employment, a list of most frequently visited places and of course, your blood type! You owe it all to them.

Applaud men for being decent human-beings
Much like rating the Uber drivers with five stars for doing their job (picking you up and dropping you off, alive and unharmed) it has become vital to praise fish for swimming, the sun for shining and men for not killing us! Praise him for being a decent man. Praise him for not being a dead-beat father or paying the bills because it is in fact a tall-order for a man to honor his responsibilities and actually follow through with what he said he would do. Questioning or challenging how he goes about doing any of these things might just threaten his position so be sure to remain silent and grateful. These are just some of the rules life has taught me. These rules, of course are just the basic fundamentals to surviving the world. These are just the starter-pack rules. What about the

rules passed down to us from our mothers, aunts and paid, full-time security guards of the patriarchy?

Sistah- Sistah rules

These are probably the most crucial rules to learn because they govern how women interact with women. These rules include; competing for the attention of men, allowing men to convince us that we are better than the woman standing next to us, accepting the endorsement of a man as validation and of course that women must hate women. They convince us that issues of jealousy or character clashes are exclusively "Women's Issues" because envy is an emotion strictly reserved for women. My favorite in this category is the "having more male friends than female friends makes you the coolest woman in the world"... to men, because "women are full of drama". The goal is to be liked by men. To be chosen by them. To be blissfully unaware that these are the very weapons of the patriarchy that convince us that the sisters next to us are the enemy. Alongside these women are the ones who have mastered this game and it's rules. The premium woman is one that is high-key selective about where and how she exercises her feminism. Still wanting to be picked by men, while fighting the good fight when it is convenient for her schedule and she is just in time to benefit from the patriarchy. If you remember nothing else, remember this; it is not cool to be a feminist next to boys.

Keep your cool when the jokes turn offensive. Breathe, count to ten while your head is about to combust. No one wants to be around that girl. The girl who calls out bad behavior, offensive jokes and stereotypes? Be cool. No one wants the girl who's going to engage men deeply on why they think it's okay to make a rape joke. Laugh with them as they laugh at you! It's funny because the joke here is you, as you sell your soul at the feet of patriarchy. I know that you aspire to not have to 'behave' and 'abide by the rules'. That you think being disobedient, an anarchist, and an outlaw is cool, but it's not. I hope you know that the women who threw the rules out the window and blazed the trail, didn't have the opportunity to walk it.

We shouldn't have to live in the confines of the patriarchy. We shouldn't have to die for not living by rules we didn't write. But here we are, serving at the feet and at every beck and call of the patriarchy. Learn the rules, Sis or become a statistic.